Who Has More?

by Lisa Trumbauer

 STECK-VAUGHN
A Harcourt Company

www.steck-vaughn.com

This boy has some puppies.

These girls have some puppies.

Who has more puppies?

These girls have some balloons.

This boy has some balloons.

Who has more balloons?

This girl has some flowers.

This boy has some flowers.

Who has more flowers?

The boy and girl have ice cream cones.

Who has more ice cream?